Flourishing Hope

a 30-day devotional for pregnant women in unexpected places

Leah Outten and Katie McCoy

KingdomWinds
PUBLISHING

Copyright © 2024 by Leah Outten and Katie McCoy

All rights reserved. No part of this publication may be reproduced, distributed, or transmitted in any form or by any means, including photocopying, recording, or other electronic or mechanical methods, without the prior written permission of the publisher, except in the case of brief quotations embodied in critical reviews and certain other noncommercial uses permitted by copyright law. For permission requests, write to the publisher at publishing@kingdomwinds.com.

Unless otherwise indicated, all Scripture references are taken from the Holy Bible, New International Version®, NIV® Copyright © 1973, 1978, 1984, 2011 by Biblica, Inc.® Used by permission. All rights reserved worldwide.

First Edition, 2024
ISBN: 978-1-64590-063-4
Published by Kingdom Winds Publishing.
www.kingdomwinds.com
publishing@kingdomwinds.com
Printed in the United States of America.

From Katie—

Dedicated to Caden and Olivia. You are the reason I find this ministry so important. You are the strength, hope, and goodness that comes from unplanned pregnancy. I love you both so very much!

From Leah—

For every mom who finds herself within the pages of this book. This is for you, my friend.

A Note from Us

As we have been praying over this devotional, we have been praying over you. We have been right there in the depths of unplanned pregnancy, just like you are right now. We pray for clarity over you as you plan for you and your baby so that you can feel confident moving forward. We pray for courage as you walk forward with purpose in the plan God has for your life. We pray you know each time you look in the mirror, Who created you and who He says you are—redeemed and made new, more precious than gems, and a beloved child of God.

On the cover, you'll see a fireweed flower. We chose this not only because of beauty but for the message it represents. The USDA Forest Service explains it this way, "The name fireweed stems from its ability to colonize areas burned by fire rapidly. It was one of the first plants to appear after the eruption of Mt. St. Helens in 1980. Known as rosebay willowherb in Great Britain, fireweed quickly colonized burned ground after the bombing of London in World War II, bringing color to an otherwise grim landscape."[1]

You see, though it feels like your world may feel shaken and burned right now, know that there will be beauty that flourishes amongst the ashes. You *will* see beauty again soon in your life. The Lord *will* bring good from this pain. The fireweed flower is a reminder to cling to God as you wade through the rubble and prepare for this new chapter of your life. There's no going back, only forward.

We pray this devotional will speak hope to your heart in this unexpected place.

Love,
Katie and Leah

---

[1] Vizgirdas, Edna. "Fireweed (Chamerion angustifulium)." Plant of the Week. U.S. Forest Service. https://www.fs.usda.gov/wildflowers/plant-of-the-week/chamerion_angustifolium.shtml

A DEVOTIONAL FOR PREGNANT WOMEN IN UNEXPECTED PLACES

Table of Contents

A Note from Us	5
DAY 1: Lament (Katie)	8
DAY 2: Do You Really Trust Him? (Leah)	10
DAY 3: When the Road Ahead Seems Terrifying (Leah)	14
DAY 4: Wait on the Lord (Katie)	18
DAY 5: Motherhood (Katie)	22
DAY 6: Sacrificial Love (Leah)	26
DAY 7: A Prayer from Mama (Katie)	30
DAY 8: Surviving the Waves (Leah)	32
DAY 9: Rejoice Always (Katie)	34
DAY 10: Dumping the Baggage (Leah)	38
DAY 11: Made Complete (Katie)	42
DAY 12: Alabaster Jars (Katie)	46
DAY 13: Perfect Peace (Leah)	50
DAY 14: Seen and Valued (Katie)	52
DAY 15: He Takes Care of Us (Katie)	56
DAY 16: Seeing the Big Picture (Leah)	58
DAY 17: Wonderfully Made (Katie)	62
DAY 18: From Broken to Special (Leah)	64
DAY 19: Where Does Help Come From? (Katie)	68
DAY 20: The Root of Bitterness (Leah)	72
DAY 21: Sound Mind (Katie)	76
DAY 22: Patience in the Process (Leah)	80
DAY 23: Refining Fires (Leah)	84
DAY 24: Heart of Worship (Katie)	88
DAY 25: New (Leah)	90
DAY 26: Steppingstones to God (Leah)	92
DAY 27: Arise (Katie)	96
DAY 28: Bloom Where You Are Planted (Leah)	98
DAY 29: He Rewrote My Story (Katie)	102
DAY 30: Receiving Blessings (Leah)	104
Closing letter	107
Acknowledgments	108
Resources	110
About Us	112

DAY 1

Lament

—Katie—

> "Come to me, all who labor and are heavy laden, and I will give you rest. Take my yoke upon you, and learn from me, for I am gentle and lowly in heart, and you will find rest for your souls. For my yoke is easy, and my burden is light."
>
> Matthew 11:28–30, ESV

I remember sitting in church one Sunday and crying silently during a sermon on Mary, mother of Jesus. It suddenly dawned on me the shame and grief Mary was facing as a pregnant woman in an unconventional situation. I felt validated by Mary, but even further, if Mary, the mother of my Savior, understood my pain, then I also have to acknowledge that Jesus knew Mary's pain. Therefore, He knows mine, too, as a woman who has had two unplanned pregnancies. He is capable of sitting in grief with us because He is familiar with it. He knows it deeply and cares for us.

After choosing to place my children for adoption, I have learned, even seventeen years down the road, that healing is not linear and that I am still lamenting not being their parent. While I don't regret the decision I made, I miss my kids a lot. I get to see them often through an open adoption plan, but I still experienced a loss, and it affects me. When I'm lost in the depths of grief, I remember that I'm deeply loved and known by the One who holds it all together. I don't have to do anything but lean on Him.

Reflect and Respond

Do you believe that your shame and grief are known by God?

Do you trust you can lean on God during grief?

What do you do when you find yourself in moments of grief? How do you cope?

What would be some new coping skills to try next time you are feeling sad?

DAY 2

Do You Really Trust Him?

—Leah—

"Trust in the Lord with all your heart and lean not on your own understanding; in all your ways submit to him, and he will make your paths straight."

Proverbs 3:5–6, NIV

"Leah, do you trust Me?"

Yes, Lord.

"But do you **really** trust me?"

We all tend to grab control of the reins of life, trusting in *our* plan instead of *His*. This particular conversation happened when I discovered I was pregnant for the seventh time. Yes, you read that right. Between having an open adoption, a miscarriage, and parenting children, I'm a mom in many different roles. I've experienced two teen pregnancies that were unintended, but the emotions during my seventh pregnancy felt very similar to those crisis situations. Even though I was years into a healthy marriage, owned a home, my career was growing, and had four children at home at the time, plus an open adoption with my oldest—I was panicking at adding more to my proverbial plate.

My plan was to be done growing our family. *My plan* was to focus on my writing more. *My plan* was to get more sleep in life!

And yes, those things did come in time. But first, God asked me to trust Him with His plan. It wasn't easy, as you know all too well right now. Sometimes, I lay in bed the most nauseous I had ever been in all my pregnancies, wondering, "Why, God?" Some days, I felt

fear that I wasn't going to be a good enough mom to all my kids and meet their emotional and physical needs.

But the Lord reassured me over and over that He was equipping me for this task He has called me to do. Did the timing and path seem off-course to me? You bet. But the truth is that God knows the best path and purpose for our lives. That just may include an additional bundle of joy we hadn't planned—but He did!

He is asking you, too, "Do you really trust Me? Do you trust My plan?"

Reflect and Respond

What are you grieving in your unexpected change of plans?

List all the ways He has been faithful in the past. Remember: He will not fail you now!

Do you think you can learn to trust God's best plan for you in this situation and to bring purpose? Write a prayer asking for help to trust Him.

DAY 3

When the Road Ahead Seems Terrifying

—Leah—

"I lift up my eyes to the mountains—where does my help come from? My help comes from the Lord, the Maker of heaven and earth."

Psalm 121:1–2, NIV

I once visited Colorado, where my mom and I booked a bus tour up to the top of Pikes Peak. To be honest, I was pretty nervous. Between the fear of altitude sickness, motion sickness of curvy roads, and fear of heights...oh...and very few guardrails, all I could think about was avoiding sickness or trusting the driver (and the protection of the Lord) to not send us crashing over the edge. I had to remind myself that we hired our driver for a reason, since he has the experience and knows the way.

As we wound up and up, around hairpin curves one after another, I remember looking up directly above us and seeing other cars doing the same thing. It looked so high above us, and I anxiously thought, "Can't we just stop and enjoy the view from here?!" Yet we pressed on...and on...and guess what? Of course, when we reached the top, the view was worth it! The beauty of God's creation from above always amazes me and reminds me just how small I am in this world.

With that visual in mind of my fear of what's ahead and climbing roads, God spoke to me. He said, "You are looking ahead in your life at what I am calling you out to do, just like watching those cars ahead. It seems high and scary right now, but I'm with you. One step at a time, one turn at a time. I am the bus driver you trust to get you there. And when you get to your destination, I will equip you

and strengthen you as I have done so far. It's all worth the work and the view for My glory. Don't worry."

Our God is a comforter and a peace-giver. I have seen time and again when God has shut doors, but His purpose is greater, and it makes sense now. Since then, He has provided step after step of opportunities that seemed scary, but I did it anyway. Steps of faith taken in obedience are often like that, right? But peace always comes when it's the right step on the right path—the one the Lord has for each of us.

So, friend, keep your eyes on the road ahead. The next curve, the next stretch, look forward to the new view. He is trustworthy to get you where His glorious plans are taking you. Lift your eyes to where your help comes from. He *will* help you!

Reflect and Respond

What are you focusing on right now that seems terrifying?

What could you focus on instead that would help release trust in your Driver (The Lord)?

A DEVOTIONAL FOR PREGNANT WOMEN IN UNEXPECTED PLACES

DAY 4

Wait on the Lord

—Katie—

"I waited patiently for the Lord to help me, and he turned to me and heard my cry."

Psalm 40:1, NLT

Have you ever watched a child fall down and then, instead of getting right back up, the child cries out for their parents because they feel defeated? I don't know about you, but almost every time that I mess up or something doesn't go as planned, I get dysregulated, and I just want someone to comfort me and make it better. But I want *instant* results. I cry out to God, "Hello! Can't You see that this isn't going how I wanted? Can't You see Your child is in pain? Lord, why would You allow this?" Sometimes, I don't get an answer, and that leaves me feeling even more discouraged and not seen by God. But yet, when I am in these places, sometimes I don't realize that I'm not even listening for God. I'm certainly not waiting or being still, so how would I catch the Father talking to me?

The Psalms use the phrase "wait on the Lord" about 25 times. David was no stranger to struggle and wrestling with the goodness of God. We see him cry out in praise, desperation, heartache, and joy all throughout Psalms. Waiting on the Lord here means to be still and listen. What is God showing me? What are His promises over my life? Who do I know God to be? Am I in a hurry and missing what God's saying to me?

In John Mark Comer's book *The Ruthless Elimination of Hurry*, he states, "Hurry is violence to the soul."[2] I wrestled with this thought the other day because I am a hustler by all definitions. I am constantly on the go, doing the most and being the most extra, and I usually think I can juggle it all well. But what quickly makes me drop the ball is when I am not spending time still and listening to God. The rest of

---

[2] Comer, John Mark. *The Ruthless Elimination of Hurry: How to Stay Emotionally Healthy and Spiritually Alive in the Chaos of the Modern World.* United States, Random House Publishing Group, 2019.

Psalm 40 shares how the Lord rescues us and gets us on our feet again. The testimonies of what He does for us will lead others to know of the goodness of God because how could we not joyfully share His greatness?

It might be hard right now to trust God and to wait on Him, but I know it will be worth it. Only He can hold it all together. Only He can make mourning turn into dancing and give hope to the hopeless. I've seen Him work wonders over many lives, and I know He can do it in yours, too. You just have to pause and let Him sit with you.

Reflect and Respond

Do you hurry through life expecting instant gratification?

Why is it important for us to pause and be present with God?

Are there things that you need to trust God with more?

A DEVOTIONAL FOR PREGNANT WOMEN IN UNEXPECTED PLACES

DAY 5

Motherhood

—Katie—

"He settles the childless woman in her home as a happy mother of children. Praise the Lord."

Psalm 113:9, NIV

You may be reading the above verse thinking, "but I am carrying a child, so what does that verse have to do with me?" An unplanned pregnancy can bring in a whirlwind of emotions and options. I wanted to spend a little time sharing how motherhood can look vastly different in many walks of life. Here are a few Biblical mothers for some inspiration; motherhood can mean so many different things, and the Lord can use it all.

Hannah is perhaps one of the most famous references when talking about infertility and waiting to conceive. Hannah so desperately wanted to be a mother. She prayed for God to give her a child and vowed to raise that child to worship God. God saw her heart and granted her Samuel, which means "God has heard."

Mary is the original poster girl for unplanned pregnancy. Ok, but seriously, she didn't ask to be pregnant, and she sure didn't expect to be pregnant, but the Lord granted her one of the most precious gifts, mothering God in the flesh. Sometimes, I think about how mind-blowing that is: Mary knew Jesus more intimately than we could ever imagine because she got to be His mom. It wasn't what she expected, but we see her adoration of her child clearly documented in Scripture. She was thankful for the unexpected. I can't wait to chat with her when I get to heaven because I know she is a wellspring of wisdom that will just help my mama heart be filled.

Motherhood comes to women in all sorts of ways, and for some women, physically bearing children will not be part

of their stories. Some adopt while others serve; whatever their stories may be, these women want to be marked by motherhood in a way that honors God. As a birth mother, I identify with these women because while I trusted God to redeem my story, I experienced a long season in which, because I was not parenting my children, I wasn't viewed as a mother. But I knew in my heart that, while it looked different for me, the title of "mother" was still part of my identity. The same is true of all women whose circumstances necessitate they approach motherhood in a different way: they are mothers, too.

No matter how motherhood comes to you or is defined in your mind, it's a special identity that God has set apart for so many incredible women historically and today! Whether your journey leads you to parenting, placing your child for adoption, or getting creative with how motherhood will be implemented in your life, remember that motherhood isn't a one-size-fits-all job description. It's all rooted in your heart.

Reflect and Respond

What defines motherhood to you?

How did you expect motherhood to look in your life?

Outside of bearing children, how could you be marked by motherhood in the future?

A DEVOTIONAL FOR PREGNANT WOMEN IN UNEXPECTED PLACES

DAY 6

Sacrificial Love

—Leah—

"Do nothing out of selfish ambition or vain conceit. Rather, in humility value others above yourselves, not looking to your own interests but each of you to the interests of the others."

Philippians 2:3–4, NIV

Being a mother is often rooted in sacrificial love. As a parent, you may wish you could go about your day as planned, but your child's needs will arise, and you have to have flexibility. You may wish you could sleep through the night, but your baby needs to be fed, so you scoop them up to snuggle and rock in the quiet of the night. So much of our time, energy, and resources spent are examples of sacrificial love.

I know as a birth mom and now mother that sacrificial love has looked different in how I mother each child and through different seasons. As a birth mom, I sacrificed my desire to parent to provide my daughter with what I felt was best for her at that time in my life. I loved her fiercely enough to trust the Lord in the steps I knew He was calling me to take, and He gave me the strength to follow His leading. That same strength from Him allowed me to change and adapt who I was to become a parenting mother a few years later. Even still with teenagers now at home, His strength helps me to joyfully sacrifice (though, to be honest, I still grumble some days) my time, money, and energy to be the mother they need.

Did you know that being pregnant means you are already a mother? Carrying your child, their simply existing within you, makes you a mother. You are already making sacrificial love decisions, not out of selfish ambition but for your child's best interest. Maybe you've given up alcohol or caffeine. Maybe you've switched fried foods for more vegetables. Maybe you'd made decisions to

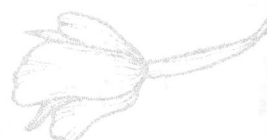

leave toxic environments to better yourself and your child's home. You are already loving your child in beautiful ways!

No matter your path ahead and where the Lord takes you, remember that Jesus first loved you with a sacrificial love. He will equip you in strength for what He has called you to do as this child's mother.

Reflect and Respond

What examples of sacrificial love have you experienced in your life?

Do you feel like it's possible to joyfully sacrifice? Why or why not?

What steps do you feel like God is calling you to take out of sacrificial love?

A DEVOTIONAL FOR PREGNANT WOMEN IN UNEXPECTED PLACES

DAY 7

A Prayer from Mama
—Katie—

Lord, I am broken. I am feeling confused and overwhelmed. I don't know what to do. This wasn't how I expected things to go. Please help me.

God, will You please keep me and my baby healthy? Will You help me find peace in the storm? Can You help me learn to trust that You have a plan for my life and my baby's life?

Lord, I ask that You give me clarity on what to do next. Only open doors I am supposed to walk through. Give me the confidence to make moves toward what's next for us. Help me feel safe.

God, I ask that as I go through this season, You will draw me closer to You. I ask that, even when it's scary or hard, I will look to You for help and answers.

I pray for my baby's future, that You will guide them through life, and that You will place people in their lives who encourage and uplift them. I trust You will protect them from harm and sickness. I pray You will grow the desire in their heart to know You.

God, I believe you are a good Father, and You want the best for our lives. Help me cling to that promise throughout my pregnancy and throughout our lives.

Amen.

A DEVOTIONAL FOR PREGNANT WOMEN IN UNEXPECTED PLACES

Reflect and Respond

Write a prayer for your baby's life.

DAY 8

Surviving the Waves
—Leah—

"When you go through deep waters, I will be with you. When you go through rivers of difficulty, you will not drown."

Isaiah 43:2a, NLT

Does your life ever feel like you're trying to enjoy a day at the beach, wanting to choose sunshine and joy, but wave after wave keeps hitting you? Those waves can be in the forms of financial struggles, a family conflict, a job loss, a death of a loved one, and yes, even a new baby. Those waves are part of life, yet sometimes it can feel unfairly too much at once.

Sometimes life feels like a giant wave for me, too. A tsunami-level wave threatening over me, bringing fear as I see it coming. Feeling like I can't do this, and I just might drown. Sometimes I feel like I'm going under and gasping for air. Grief does that. Change does that. Anxiety does that. How do we stay standing when the waves hit? How do we survive?

I had a dream one night that while water rushed all around me in a tsunami-flood way, and even took the lives of some people around me, God protected me. Those who trusted in the Lord survived...because they suddenly had the ability to jump the waves like a dolphin. Ha!

While I know this sounds silly, and quite honestly, it looked silly in my dream, like a very bad CGI effect, it gave me peace. It was a reminder that though there will be waves in all of our lives, in our country, in our families...there will be waves of struggle and heartache that attempt to take us down...yet He is with us. He equips us to jump those waves! *That is how we survive*—with His supernatural peace and protection, much like the supernatural ability to jump the waves in my dream. Whatever wave you are facing right now, trust God that He will keep you afloat. He's got you.

Reflect and Respond

What waves are you facing right now? What fears and anxiety are you worrying about today?

How have you seen God help you "jump waves" in your past? Take a minute to remember His goodness and how He has answered prayers before. This will help you trust Him through these new waves!

DAY 9

Rejoice Always
—Katie—

"Rejoice in the Lord always; again I will say, rejoice."

Philippians 4:4, ESV

"Rejoice in the Lord always, and again I say rejoice. Rejoice! Rejoice! Again I say rejoice!"[3] You likely know the song, but as much as I sing it over and over again, sometimes I just really don't feel capable of rejoicing. Life can be really hard, and I can't always find joy in the storms. I'll be honest with you, some of the hardest times of my life, I was running from God. I wasn't praising Him. I was trying to get out of the shadow of the "perfect Christian girl" I thought everyone expected me to be. Especially God.

I quickly found myself in very scary and difficult situations. I was running the streets and doing things I never would wish on anyone else. The problem is that we live in a broken world, and it's tricky and seductive. I thought that chasing boys, partying, and couch hopping was the key to happiness. I ended up 18, pregnant, and really scared. I remember having such tunnel vision; I was so afraid, but I felt like I could parent.

I worked really hard going to school and holding two jobs, and I was talking about marriage with my boyfriend at the time. I thought I had it all figured out. I ended up marrying that boyfriend from the part of my life that really wasn't good, and sure enough, 28 days later, I was kicking him out and asking for a divorce because he became abusive. Everything I thought I controlled came crashing down around me, and I was scrambling to pick up the pieces. I was far from rejoicing.

Fast forward 6 months, and I realize that I was not succeeding at parenting like I knew my son deserved. I chose to let my parents adopt him. I was devastated and, again, not rejoicing. 3 years

---

[3] Anonymous hymn based on Philippians 4:4.

later, I found out I was pregnant again. With the knowledge of what I had already been through, I chose to make an adoption plan. Fast forward through a LOT of ups and downs: I still struggled to rejoice. I wanted to scream at God, "Why do I have to experience so much pain?!" I knew I made the choices, but I still felt like I went through an unfair amount of suffering. But Jesus was still present.

Slowly, I began to realize how much I was provided for in all those years of suffering. To be honest with you, I rejoice today that God protected me throughout those years. I rejoice that I was able to give life to my brilliant children. I rejoice that I survived toxic relationships, substance abuse, and homelessness. I rejoice that I was constantly pursued by God. I rejoice because even in all of my brokenness, God has favored me and blessed me. We all face disappointment, trials, and hurt, but that doesn't make God any less good. When things get hard around me, I will continue to rejoice in Him, even if I don't feel like it, because He has never stopped loving me.

Reflect and Respond

What does rejoicing God look like to you?

When things are hard, we struggle to see goodness. What has He done for your life that is worthy of rejoicing in Him?

A DEVOTIONAL FOR PREGNANT WOMEN IN UNEXPECTED PLACES

DAY 10

Dumping the Baggage

—Leah—

"He will again have compassion on us; he will tread our iniquities underfoot. You will cast all our sins into the depths of the sea."

Micah 7:19, ESV

I didn't have an easy childhood, which led to difficult teen years, which then created baggage of shame that I carried around for years. This baggage consisted of both choices I had made myself and things done to me. I felt ashamed of my actions and blamed myself for the choices of others. *Why didn't I stop it? Why did I do? I'm dirty. I'm a bad person. I can't believe I did that.* My skin would crawl with disgust at the stinky trash of my past.

It's a weight that can make you feel stuck or slow-moving in life. You wish it would go away, or at least lighten to make your life easier. It's emotional baggage that feels like it is dragging behind you from year to year, relationship to relationship. The baggage of shame skews your perspective of yourself, situations, and of God. Shame lies to us about who we are, making us feel unworthy as we forget this is exactly why we have a Savior! He died for us to no longer carry around shame and to give us freedom. He makes us redeemed and worthy.

Despite knowing the Lord for many years, I was still self-blaming and so ashamed of pieces of my past. In therapy one day, I was working through processing some trauma, and I clearly felt the Lord with me. I saw in my mind's eye a black trash bag, tied up, and sinking to the bottom of the ocean. I heard Him say, "This is trash; you don't need it anymore."

Perhaps that is you, too. Maybe you have a relationship with the Lord but are still struggling with shame.

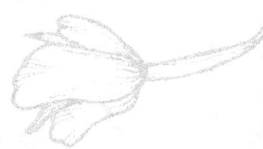

Or maybe you haven't yet truly experienced His grace and freedom. Either way, shame is baggage that the Lord doesn't intend for you to carry any longer. Handing it over to Him frees us. His Word tells us He casts our sins into the depths of the sea (Micah 7:19)! Not just to the sea, but *"as far as the east is from the west, so far does he remove our transgressions from us"* (Psalm 103:12, ESV). The East and West can never meet up; it goes on forever. It's gone.

> "So if the Son sets you free, you will be free indeed."
>
> John 8:36, ESV

Reflect and Respond

What baggage is weighing you down? Close your eyes and see what the Lord brings to mind. Write a prayer to release this baggage to Him:

DAY 11

Made Complete

—Katie—

"For I am confident of this very thing, that He who began a good work in you will perfect it until the day of Christ Jesus."

Philippians 1:6, LSB

I participate in Toastmasters, a club to help people grow as public speakers, and during one of our meetings, we received this speech prompt: *What would you tell your ten-year-old self if you could go back today?*

This hit me hard as I had been struggling and learning when trauma began to speak lies into my heart about my identity. I realized it was when I was in fifth grade, so about ten years old. I can remember details about almost everything; even my family says I have an incredible memory. Yet it's puzzling...I cannot remember fifth grade. I remember before and after, but as hard as I try, I cannot remember the details of that part of my life. I know that was the beginning of my struggle with my worth. My entire life I have wrestled with thoughts like, *where does my identity lie?* Or, *what am I really worth?* In hindsight, looking at the choices I made that led me down some really dark roads full of sin and shame, I can tell you I did not believe I had much worth, if any. As an adult, I am heartbroken for that girl. What on earth did she go through so young to begin asking the world to define her worth? How badly I desire to advise her with something like this excerpt from *Without Rival* by Lisa Bevere:

> "The truth is you are beautiful because our God beautifies the meek with salvation (Ps. 149:4). You are beautiful because God makes all things beautiful in their time (Eccles. 3:11). Do not allow the foolish idols and image makers of what the world calls beauty to speak into your life when God has already spoken blessing over your life!"

I know that, while these words hold truth and are so powerful, *that 10-year-old would have just as much difficulty walking in that truth as this 36-year-old does.*

One of my favorite books of the Bible is Hosea. I see so much of myself in Gomer, Hosea's wife. Short version: Hosea is married to Gomer, who is a prostitute and adulteress. She bears him children but then leaves him, and she's eventually auctioned off as a slave. God tells Hosea to go and get his wife. So, Hosea buys her back in the auction and pays for what's already his! This story is an illustration of God's love for us. We are covered in our shame and mess, but He pursues us no matter how dirty we become. His love is unfailing and full of grace.

> "People who would tie you to your past...have yet to experience a revelation of God's mercy and the power of the rebirth...it was the darkest, dirtiest places of my life that were later redeemed to become my deepest wells."
>
> –Lisa Bevere

I struggle with this concept every. single. day. I know fully that I am who I am because of Who He is. And that is beauty. But it is so easy for Satan to beat me down with my self-worth issues. I learned that "Gomer" in Hebrew means *complete*. Let that sink in... this woman who is sinning left and right on that hot-mess-express-train-wreck *is complete*. How gracious is that?! I can be at my most filthy, but He will always come and meet me where I am and love me with an endless love. Friends, I hope that this encourages you as much as it does me because on days like today, I need that reminder that I AM COMPLETE exactly as I am because I am His.

Reflect and Respond

Do you tend to run from God when you mess up?

You are complete in Christ, no matter what you do. How does that make you feel?

DAY 12

Alabaster Jars

—Katie—

> "And a woman in the town who was a sinner found out that Jesus was reclining at the table in the Pharisee's house. She brought an alabaster jar of perfume and stood behind him at his feet, weeping, and began to wash his feet with her tears. She wiped his feet with her hair, kissing them and anointing them with the perfume."
>
> Luke 7:37-38, CSB

I remember when I was pregnant with my firstborn I would feel the most judgment at church. I grew up in the church during the purity movement of the 1990s and early 2000s. I knew my pregnancy was a scandal; people were talking. Even if they weren't judging me, they looked at me with pity. I remember feeling so dirty and out of place. Here I was, this girl who everyone thought was such a good little Christian, pregnant out of wedlock.

We can have high expectations of others, and it can be truly unfair. I used to think—*"Well, if God's children see me this way, imagine how God must feel about me right now."*

Do you ever wonder that? Is God upset with my situation? Does He think less of me?

In Luke, there's a story about a woman with a reputation. I'm not talking about the Taylor Swift kind; I mean the lady-of-the-night kind. She takes the most precious thing she owns, her perfume stored in an alabaster jar, and goes to visit Jesus. I imagine her terrified and wrecked with anxious thoughts, wondering if she made a big mistake showing up to see Him. I mean, she knows He is aware of her sins, and it would be easy to hide instead of plop down at His feet. "Hey Jesus, it's me—the talk of the town."

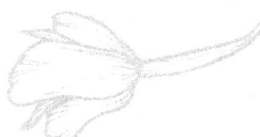

    The Pharisees and those around them were mind-blown that she was one, in their presence, but two, that Jesus was letting her wash His feet. She wept and cleaned His feet with her hair, and she anointed Him with her valuable perfume. Jesus saw Her intimate act of worship, and He blessed her in front of everyone. He declared her forgiven of all of her sins, saying that her act of service glorified Him. She wasn't too dirty for the Savior of the world—and you and I aren't either.

    Your unexpected pregnancy is not something for which you remain in shame. God knew it was going to be a part of your story, and He loves you just the same. God does not remember your sins; they're as far as the East is from the West (Psalm 103:12). You are worthy of sitting at His feet, and there is no shame in His presence. Take everything you're storing up in those alabaster jars and give it to Him. Let Him fully know you.

Reflect and Respond

What are you storing up in alabaster jars that you're scared to give to Jesus?

The woman who washed his feet experienced true worship. How do you worship God?

He has already forgiven you for your past. Can you forgive yourself?

A DEVOTIONAL FOR PREGNANT WOMEN IN UNEXPECTED PLACES

DAY 13

Perfect Peace

—Leah—

"You will keep the mind that is dependent on you in perfect peace, for it is trusting in you."

Isaiah 26:3, CSB

When I was pregnant with my first daughter, I spent much of my pregnancy lacking peace. I felt tossed back and forth like a boat caught in a storm, conflicted over decisions I needed to make. Along with physical morning sickness, the internal tossing about kept my stomach unsettled for months. Nothing felt like the right way to navigate my inner storm. I was swayed back and forth by different opinions of others and by my own desires. It wasn't until I truly stopped to pray and ask the Lord—and listen to what He said—that I found peace in my situation. I finally felt peace to move forward with the plan He had given me.

Maybe your situation right now feels the same, like a raging storm within your heart, a battle between your heart and head, a battle at the crossroads of decisions. I can't tell you what your path will be—that's between you and the Lord—but I can tell you where to find peace. Perfect peace, a supernatural peace that surpasses all understanding, is available to you, too (Philippians 4:7).

Seek Him. Ask Him. Keep your mind on Him, even when voices are saying otherwise. Depend on Him to supply every need as He guides your steps. Trusting Him brings you perfect peace, just as Isaiah wrote thousands of years ago.

A DEVOTIONAL FOR PREGNANT WOMEN IN UNEXPECTED PLACES

Reflect and Respond

What storm circumstances are going on around you today?

In what ways can you keep your mind on Him, rather than the voices around you?

Write a prayer to the Lord seeking His perfect peace:

DAY 14

Seen and Valued

—Katie—

"Are not five sparrows sold for two pennies? And not one of them is forgotten before God. Why, even the hairs of your head are all numbered. Fear not; you are of more value than many sparrows."

Luke 12:6–7, ESV

Every morning on my commute, I pass a man who volunteers as a cross guard for an elementary school. For years, I have watched this man look at every car and wave. He's consistent. No matter my mood, when he waves at me—I feel valued, and I wave back. His steadfast attention to those around him reminds me of the attention we receive from our Father. He is such a good father.

Have you ever gone through your day noticing little things that just perfectly line up or happen that make you feel acknowledged? There will be really good days where I just look around me and think, if I could have curated moments to make the perfect day, this would be it.

Guess what? God does that. He puts people, things, and moments in our path to encourage us and remind us He is the narrator and pays attention to our story.

That seems crazy to me. I am one of billions of people in the world, billions of His creation. How does He know my story, let alone my name!? I think sometimes we forget He created us with such detail, and we are so unique. How could He not remember us? He pours His heart out to us daily; we are so cherished by Him.

But what about when things don't go right? Does that come from Him, too? Does He cause the bad stuff? Romans 8:28 tells us, *"And we know that in all things God works for the good of those who love him, who have been called according to his purpose"* (NIV). All things God works for the good. Even when things

are not going well, God is working on our behalf. He is putting people in our path to help hold us up. He is placing opportunities for provision or safety. He is putting moments of laughter and goodness in to show us hope and so much more.

I will be honest: sometimes I cannot see it. I feel like I know He is supposed to be helping me and present, but the situation can be so overwhelming. Even in those moments, God is working. He is pouring out His love on you. I pray that no matter what your situation is, you will see God's goodness in the big and small things.

Reflect and Respond

How do you know God is good?

What "coincidences" have happened in your life that helped you feel seen?

Write out a prayer for what you need Him to help you with today:

DAY 15

He Takes Care of Us

—Katie—

"I will be the same until your old age, and I will bear you up when you turn gray. I have made you, and I will carry you; I will bear and rescue you."

Isaiah 46:4, CSB

I'm an early bird. In fact, I'm always the first one in the office. One morning I heard a tap, tap on my window. It surprised me because the office was nice and quiet, and I was easing into my workday. That tap quickly got more aggressive and became thuds. I figured out that there was a female cardinal trying to get into my window. This bird relentlessly continued to tap on every window of the office for *hours*. I prayed over that sweet bird because I couldn't understand why she kept doing something bad for her. Jesus said not to worry about the sparrows, but He didn't mention the mama cardinal with the sore beak y'all. (He meant her, too though, Matthew 6:26/Matthew 10:29). No matter how hard I prayed, she kept trying to go through the window.

She's been around for weeks now, which has given me plenty of time to reflect on something she reminds me of—*me*. How often have I rebelled? How often have I said, "I know you're for me, Lord, but I can't measure up—so I'm going to keep doing things my way"? Wow. I felt like I couldn't ever be who God wanted me to be, so I kept hitting windows, trying to figure it out on my own. Until finally, I realized I was who He wanted all along: a broken girl in need of a loving Father. I began to lean on Him and trust that His ways were better. And did I still mess up? Oh yes, all the time! And I'm sure just like I fret over the cardinal, The Lord shakes His head when I go hitting windows thinking my way is better, but He is so patient, and He lets me figure it out so I can come back to Him and lay it at His feet. All He wants is for us to depend on Him because He sustains us more than food, drink, or things can, and His way is always better for us.

Reflect and Respond

How have you been trying to do things your way instead of God's?

Do you believe that God really will take care of you?

What are some of the "windows" you've been hitting that might be God gently reminding you to let Him take over?

DAY 16

Seeing the Big Picture
—Leah—

"'For my thoughts are not your thoughts, neither are your ways my ways,' declares the Lord."

Isaiah 55:8, NIV

Have you ever wished you could zoom out above your situation and see the big picture? Or, like reading a book, you wish you could flip to the last chapter and see how it all works out in the end? I know I have. We often want to know exactly what will happen. We want to have control or at least a clue that it'll all be okay.

How will this turn out? What is the right choice?

In times of uncertainty and in waiting, it can be so difficult to have peace when we are wrapped up in worry. Sometimes, it can feel like God isn't answering our prayers because no visible movement is happening. Yet, throughout the Bible, we see He is always working, even in silence. He tells us that His ways are not our ways. He works through painful and uncertain experiences to not only draw us to Him but to weave together good. He is a redeemer! It just may not look how we think it will. Bad things still happen in our fallen world, yet He always uses them for good.

Think of Moses' mother, Jochebed, who, because of the decree by law to kill baby boys, felt her only option to save her son was to release him into the river in a basket. Yet, God used this to place Moses in the very palace of the Pharaoh who made this evil decree, where he was adopted and thrived! This painful moment set Moses up within God's plan, and he became a famous faith figure. He not only was spared his life by his biological and adoptive mother, but he paved the way to save Israelites from Egypt's captivity. I'm betting when Jochebed placed him into the river she wished she could "skip to the good part" and know what would happen. *Would he*

survive? Would he be taken care of well? Would she see him again? I can only imagine the depths of fear she felt in this uncertain time.

Even the best-laid plans can come with unexpected twists. Yet the Lord tells us in Jeremiah 29:11, *"For I know the plans I have for you...plans to prosper you and not to harm you, plans to give you hope and a future"* (NIV). This was a verse I clung to while pregnant. So, today when you wish you could zoom out, try to reframe your thoughts. Trust Him with being the author of your story. Trust that while you can't see the ending of this chapter in your life yet, He can!

His thoughts and ways are not our ways. Often that is evident after the fact, when we can see the big picture better.

Reflect and Respond

Has there been a time in the past when you thought something would go as planned, but it turned out very differently?

Have you ever seen God make something even better than you could have planned?

What are you struggling with today in this chapter of your story? What do you wish you could zoom out and see right now?

A DEVOTIONAL FOR PREGNANT WOMEN IN UNEXPECTED PLACES

DAY 17

Wonderfully Made

—Katie—

"For you created my inmost being; you knit me together in my mother's womb. I praise you because I am fearfully and wonderfully made; your works are wonderful, I know that full well."

Psalm 139:13-14,

Have you ever worked really hard on an art project? Or maybe you put a lot of detail into a work project? We house-hunted for over a year before finally finding a place to call home. While we didn't know it at the time, the house quickly became a project. We've worked hard to fix it up and to make it beautiful. There are so many memories in each room, even just in the two years we have owned the house. Our latest project was putting a nursery together. Sometimes I sit in that room thinking about how it came together: we painted the walls during a miscarriage bereavement and then started curating decor and furniture when we found out we were pregnant again with a baby girl. Now, it's a beautiful room that represents beauty that came from very mixed emotions. I can't wait to watch my baby grow up in not just that room but the whole house. Completing things with great care is fulfilling, but the true masterpiece is us—humans.

God put great care in creating you, and He's perfectly making your child while in your womb. He knows every detail of your life, how you'll laugh, your talents, what brings you joy, and what makes you deeply sad. He doesn't miss a single detail. You are fearfully and wonderfully made. To be treasured.

Friend, take heart. God is so passionate about caring for you in all the big and small things. You are His greatest creation, and He wants to see you thrive like any parent does. That means even in your most overwhelming seasons like you might be in now. God is for you, and He wants good things for your future.

Reflect and Respond

When you look in the mirror, do you see all the unique details that God made you to have?

God says we are more precious than rubies, but the world shares a version of women that seems really unattainable. Do you struggle to see your beauty?

When you think of your child, what dreams do you have for them?

DAY 18

From Broken to Special

—Leah—

"Behold, I will do something new, Now it will spring forth; Will you not know it? I will even make a roadway in the wilderness, Rivers in the wasteland."

Isaiah 43:19, LSB

I was once told by an organization, "What makes you special is that you've walked both paths of choosing life. You've chosen adoption, and you've been a teen mom. You have a lot of experience to share."

Let me tell you, when I was 16 and 19, I didn't feel special. I felt broken. I felt like my life was over. I felt like I had let my family down—twice—and I was a failure. I was a mess. I knew I was going to walk forward in faith, but I didn't know how it would all turn out or when the weight on my heart would lift. It was the darkest, most hard months of my life. Can you relate?

But God.

But for the lives of my beautiful girls who are here 20 and 17 years later. My daughter still tells me, fully aware that I had options, "Thank you for giving birth to me."

God shows up to remind us that our pain has purpose. His plan is for *good and much bigger than us. The story He's authored over me makes me special. He has made all things new. He has breathed life into* what was dead within me. He has written chapters of redemption that I'm living out today.

Friend, the story He is writing for you is special, too. You are worthy of that! Trust His plan, even when it's dark. Even when you are sitting in the muck of a place where you feel stuck forever. Let our stories here serve as hope. When we trust in Him to get us out, He will. Maybe it's not today. Maybe He has some pruning and rearranging to do first, but He will.

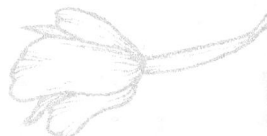

One day, when you are on the other side of this season and you see all that God has done to make things new in your life, I pray you will use your voice and story for His glory, too.

Reflect and Respond

In what ways do you feel broken today?

What do you hope God will restore and redeem in the future?

How might your story bring purpose to your life one day?

A DEVOTIONAL FOR PREGNANT WOMEN IN UNEXPECTED PLACES

DAY 19

Where Does Help Come From?

—Katie—

"The Lord watches over you—the Lord is your shade at your right hand; the sun will not harm you by day, nor the moon by night."

Psalm 121: 5–6, NIV

Last night, my husband was reading his Bible and said to me, "This is my prayer for you and our child." He then began to read me Psalm 121. I've heard it many times before, but hearing my husband speak that over me and our unborn child gave new light to words I have read a million times. It also made me reflect.

Where does my help come from? If I am being honest, I would answer that with, "I don't know that help always comes. It sure hasn't felt like it in my life lately." I've shared in previous devotions that my husband and I have had some hardships at the beginning of our marriage, and as a birth mother who has placed children for adoption, I am no stranger to painful and challenging moments. But lately, it feels like every time we get a win, the devil is right there to kick us back down. It's frustrating and disheartening.

But maybe I'm too busy focusing on the unfairness of it all to see God working right before me. I love how David says, "The Lord is your shade at your right hand." If you think about the shade or a shadow, we know that the light has to line up with an object or person in order to cast a shadow. This illustration struck me as another sign of God's goodness. If the Lord is the shade at my right hand, then the light of God must be cast upon me always. And sweet friend, while this illustration is a beautiful picture of our ever-present Father, the truth is

He never stops working behind the scenes, moving on our behalf, and loving us as a father does. Even when we can't see it, God is lining up the goodness, provision, protection, and help. We just have to trust Him to reveal His plan in His timing.

Reflect and Respond

Think back to the last time you felt helpless. Can you think of any ways God showed up for you in that moment, or even after?

How have you seen God be your shade and protection lately?

Have you been able to easier trust the Lord to be your help?

A DEVOTIONAL FOR PREGNANT WOMEN IN UNEXPECTED PLACES

DAY 20

The Root of Bitterness

—Leah—

"Watch out that no poisonous root of bitterness grows up to trouble you, corrupting many."

Hebrews 12:15b, NLT

Have you ever thought of your heart and mind like a garden? I dream of a heart that is beautiful, pure, and full of joy–like a wildflower garden with bright colors and sweet fruit trees. Yet, quickly into my daily life, I can spot a weed pushing its way through, trying to choke out goodness and beauty. It takes form in the way I respond to my youngest with an angry snap when she whines instead of with empathy. Or, in how a person's mean comment affects my mood for the whole day as my self-esteem falters.

Hurt people hurt people. Often that's because of this deep bitterness root. It may feel good for a minute to lash out, but does it help? Nope. It only makes the root grow deeper, entangling us even more.

The root of bitterness can be a tough one to rip out for a healthy garden of the soul and mind. It doesn't just affect you; it affects the people around you: how we react, how we may interact with others, even those undeserving of the bitter treatment we give. It can choke out the fruit and good things God is trying to grow in and around us.

So, how do we uproot bitterness so beauty can grow again?

Forgiveness—of our own faults and of others. Grace—extended to ourselves and to others. That's what releases the root. It will be a process, taking one forgiving act and one root at a time. Just like kneeling into real soil, grabbing one handful of weeds at a time. Repeating, over and over, until it's cleared. But it can be done, especially with God's help! Ask Him. After all, He is the Master Gardener.

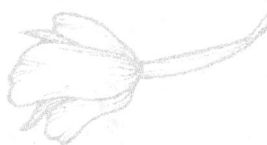

Relationships are not easy, and growth isn't easy. I promise I'm right there with you, praying and pulling roots from the soil of my heart's garden. It may never be perfect, as new weeds and life experiences pop up on this side of Heaven, but pulling them out and taking each root to the feet of Lord will help keep them maintained!

Reflect and Respond

What is your vision of a healthy heart and mind garden?

List people and circumstances that have hurt you below. Then, pray over this list and ask God to help you pull up the bitterness rooted with each.

What do you feel God is calling you to do with these roots? What is one step you can take to begin to release the bitterness?

A DEVOTIONAL FOR PREGNANT WOMEN IN UNEXPECTED PLACES

DAY 21

Sound Mind

—Katie—

"Therefore, I remind you to keep ablaze the gift of God that is in you through the laying on of my hands. For God has not given us a spirit of fearfulness, but one of power, love, and sound judgment."

2 Timothy 1:6-7, HCSB

Paul can always be counted on for a good message, y'all. In 2 Timothy 1, he's writing a letter to his spiritual son, Timothy. He loves Timothy, and Paul sees how phenomenal he is. But he also sees that Timothy is afraid and timid and that it's holding him back from walking in the fullness of God's truth over his life. I love when the Bible is so transparent with us and reminds us that even the OG's (original gangsters, for those who aren't holy and hood like me) of following Jesus were still vulnerable humans who didn't have it all figured out. God is so kind to remind us that even the people who walked beside Jesus (God in the flesh right in front of them!) struggled.

One morning, I was listening to my worship music on the way to work, and I was praying over my husband and myself. We got married last year and immediately started trying to have a baby. I had this expectation that we'd get pregnant fast, but 9 months later, I was labeled with secondary infertility. I have been wrestling with God. It just didn't seem fair. I had birthed two kids whom I placed for adoption, and I feared not being able to parent one someday. But God was so sweet to me that morning, and I heard Him say, "I know it's unfair and hard, but that fear is not from me." It was an ah-ha moment for me because while it seems like a simple concept that "God is for us, not against us," it's hard to wrap our hearts around.

Just like Timothy, I tend to get caught up in fear, especially when it involves a lack of control. Fear can arrest my mind,

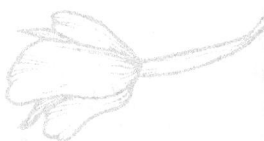

and I get lost in grief. I become isolated from God, and I let the enemy plant fear and lies in my head. I forget God's promises to me. I forget that He is good to us. Take a look at The Message's version of Romans 8:28:

> "Meanwhile, the moment we get tired in the waiting, God's Spirit is right alongside helping us along. If we don't know how or what to pray, it doesn't matter. He does our praying in and for us, making prayer out of our wordless sighs, our aching groans. He knows us far better than we know ourselves, knows our pregnant condition, and keeps us present before God. That's why we can be so sure that every detail in our lives of love for God is worked into something good."
>
> Romans 8:26–28, MSG

I love how this passage encompasses the fact that even when life isn't apparently good, God still is. And because we love Him, we can rest on the truth that He will take our fears and doubts and make something good. We may not see the results quickly or even at all, but He can work them into something good.

Reflect and Respond

What fears are you clinging to?

How can you maintain a sound mind, rejecting thoughts that are not true?

What's keeping you from laying it down for Jesus to work out?

A DEVOTIONAL FOR PREGNANT WOMEN IN UNEXPECTED PLACES

DAY 22

Patience in the Process

—Leah—

> "Be patient, then, brothers and sisters, until the Lord's coming. See how the farmer waits for the land to yield its valuable crop, patiently waiting for the autumn and spring rains. You too, be patient and stand firm, because the Lord's coming is near."
>
> James 5:7-8, NIV

One of my daughters handed me back the dense, green pear with a bite out of it and a disgusted look on her face. "It's not sweet. Why is it not sweet yet?" I responded with, "That's because it isn't ripe yet; that's why I suggested you wait another day or two for it to be sweet." For her, it was a lesson of ripening fruit, and in a few more days, she enjoyed another pear that was sweet and ready. She was delighted!

For me, God used this lesson of a pear's process to remind me of His timing and my own impatience. We all have a fleshy desire to rush ahead in the process, to want something *now* and question "Why?" when it isn't happening in our own timeline. Unfortunately, this is a repeated pattern in my life and a lesson I often have to be gently reminded of by the Lord.

I have grumbled through the years like waiting for my (now) husband to propose, as I begged labor to start, and as I wondered if we would ever find the perfect house. Still today, despite His answering past prayers, I can have moments of frustration as I wonder when God will bless my efforts. When will it be time?

We can get a glimpse of the good promises ahead that God has for us, and we want fulfillment now. We want the sweet fruit now. But God's ways are not our ways (Isaiah 55:8–9)! He has His process and timing for a purpose—to grow us, strengthen our faith, and teach us patience. I'm in a season again of "Why, God? When will this happen?" I've been frustrated, downhearted, and

even a bit bitter some days. And then God used this little green pear and my child to remind me, "I've got this. Trust Me. The time for sweet will come. Patience, child." And so, I pray if you are in a season of waiting too, you will trust in His timing. Let it anchor your soul to hope and comfort in the wait. Like His timing of a ripened fruit, the season of waiting will end, and sweet blessings will come.

Reflect and Respond

What prayer or promise are you waiting on today?

What might God be teaching you in this season of waiting for His promise for you?

A DEVOTIONAL FOR PREGNANT WOMEN IN UNEXPECTED PLACES

DAY 23

Refining Fires
—Leah—

"When you walk through fire you shall not be burned, and the flame shall not consume you."

Isaiah 43:2b, ESV

In previous days, we talked about the first part of this verse when God is with us through the rising waters of life. Today I wanted to focus on the second part of the verse. I know that I *always* need the reminder that God is with me in all circumstances. I figured you might need that encouragement again, too. Not only that, but we need to remember that there is purpose through these difficult times, and beauty can come from them, just like those fireweed flowers after a forest fire.

Many times throughout the Bible, refining metals is used as a metaphor for how God uses trials in our lives to refine us. One example is found in Psalm 66:10: *"For you, God, tested us; you refined us as silver is refined"* (CSB). And again in Isaiah 48:10: *"Look, I have refined you, but not as silver; I have tested you in the furnace of affliction"* (CSB).

I know the proverbial furnaces and fires of afflictions are not comfortable. No one *wants* to be in this unexpected place. No one *wants* to walk through painful situations. Yet, it is part of being human. Just as physical growth often has stretching pains, so can the mind and soul when it is maturing. The process of refining is important in life; it has a purpose.

Why is refining metals important? It creates purity. When gold or silver is mined, it has impurities within it. As it melts over the fire, the impurities rise to the top to be removed. Similarly, the fires of life purify our hearts and help us become more and more like Jesus. Trials teach us life lessons about the very things we've been walking through together in this devotional—about trust,

beginning and maturing our faith, forgiveness, and grace. Katie and I don't have it all down perfectly, I can assure you! We are still growing in our faith and being purified, too. We all will until the day we die. But what we've shared in this devotional are personal experiences of our fires in life and how God has used them to teach us and bring out of them.

I know you may feel surrounded by fire right now. I know you may be standing in ashes and smoke as the life you imagined living changes into something else entirely. But today, I pray you take hope knowing that you will not be consumed by these fires because He is with you. He is teaching you. And He will bring beauty from these ashes. Keep trusting Him through the refining process, my friend.

Reflect and Respond

What "fire" circumstance feels like it will consume you today?

What might the Lord be refining in your life through these trials? How have you seen growth in yourself?

Write a prayer to the Lord leaning into His protection and plan through your fires:

DAY 24

Heart of Worship

—Katie—

"I have seen you in your sanctuary and gazed upon your power and glory. Your unfailing love is better than life itself; how I praise you! I will praise you as long as I live, lifting up my hands to you in prayer."

Psalm 63:2-4, NLT

I have been singing since I was a little girl. I grew up performing and have always felt comfortable on stage. As I've gotten older, anxiety has crept into the most unexpected places. I'm on the worship team at church, and I remember one day getting super anxious before a set. I couldn't comprehend why something I'd been doing forever so confidently was suddenly a cause for panic and fear of rejection. I had to not only begin to lean on the Lord to provide for me in those times, but to really unpack what worship meant to me. Worship is the most intimate act of praise. I can literally feel the Holy Spirit all around me when I'm singing to God. Nothing else matters, just being in His presence.

What takes you to the throne room? For some people, it's nature. It's hard not to look around at creation and not feel closer to the Creator. Worship doesn't have to be where you turn on some Kari Jobe (but GIRL, she can take me to church); it can be in journaling, reading the Bible or doing a devotional, walking in nature, praying, talking to Jesus, serving others, etc. You see, worship is not in the act, but rather in the posture of our hearts.

I always feel better after worshiping. I am able to see so clearly who God has made me to be and where He is pointing me in life, and I hear Him throughout the day so much better. My heart for Him is blessed with His goodness in my life. Even when things are hard, I can always depend on Him to show up when I am coming with a heart of worship. I hope He continues to bless you and puts big and small things in your path to remind you of His goodness. You are such a treasure to Him.

Reflect and Respond

How do you worship God?

Take a few minutes to worship (we have a playlist in the back!), and as you do, write what God reveals to you here:

DAY 25

New

—Leah—

"He who was seated on the throne said, 'I am making everything new!' Then he said, 'Write this down, for these words are trustworthy and true.'"

Revelation 21:5, NIV

If you're anything like me, you have a past. Those yucky parts of our story, the old version of us and the character traits we didn't like that used people, lied, or manipulated. The shame can be paralyzing, sometimes making us feel unworthy of anything good.

Yet trusting in Jesus means He washes us clean and makes us new. Like a shepherd whose lamb lost its way into a muddy path full of briars, Jesus rescues us and cleans us back up. When shame tries to sneak back and remind you who you used to be, counter those shameful lies with this truth:

"Therefore, if anyone is in Christ, the new creation has come: The old has gone, the new is here!"

2 Corinthians 5:17–18, NIV

Maybe you don't feel new yet. Maybe you have been hesitant to fully trust Jesus. Remember, this is also a promise to those who don't see or feel this yet. It's a process. It may not (will not) fully happen on this earth, but He is faithful to keep His promises (Psalm 145:13). Keep trusting Him, clinging to Him, obeying Him when He says to stop or make a move, and He will make things new in your life. If He can raise Jesus from the dead, part the Red Sea, change Christian-killing Saul into Jesus-following Paul, He can make things new for you too—and what a story of glory that will be!

There is so much hope of a new beginning, of healing, of beauty rising from your story, too.

A DEVOTIONAL FOR PREGNANT WOMEN IN UNEXPECTED PLACES

Reflect and Respond

What kind of person did you used to be?

In what ways has the Lord made you new?

How does the promise of making things new bring you hope for what is possible in your life?

DAY 26

Steppingstones to God

—Leah—

"Be to me a rock of refuge, to which I may continually come; you have given the command to save me, for you are my rock and my fortress."

Psalm 71:3, ESV

I didn't have an easy childhood, and it led me down a path toward destructive choices—and to unplanned pregnancies. Maybe that's your story, too. I was sexually abused by at least two men as a child and struggled with my worth for a long time. For many years, after I realized what I was a victim of and as I was working through healing, I kept crying out to God, "Where were you? Why didn't you stop him?!" I felt that all of this pain could have been avoided. I blamed the men. I blamed my family life circumstances. I blamed God for not stopping it or changing the story. I felt Him present with me in the moment, but not in my past. My abuse led me to feel like God wasn't a good father or a protector, but an absent one. This was a lie from the enemy, not truth. It was a stumbling block I kept tripping over in my journey because my eyes were focused on the wrong perspective.

Then one day my therapist asked me, "What is your story? Tell me the events that lead you to know Jesus." So I did, from the painful parts of my childhood to my unplanned pregnancy and adoption decision at 16, to the beautiful redemption that has become our life. She then asked, "Could the beautiful parts of your story have happened without the painful beginning?"

Thoughtfully, I considered her question and realized it wasn't possible. If I hadn't had the family I grew up in, hadn't been abused, hadn't dated a jerky guy, hadn't had my daughter...I wouldn't have this story and wouldn't know Him as personally as I do now. He was with me through it all, from every painfully humbling

low to the beautiful mountaintop healing moments that led me closer to His presence and healing. He wasn't absent through it all; He was right beside me, guiding my steps toward Him! Each pain point was a steppingstone towards the Lord, a part of my story that led me to a higher and better place, one greater than I could have imagined.

The Bible uses the image of rocks in two different ways: a stumbling block or a solid rock, a foundation. The Lord is often referred to as our solid rock and our foundation. In contrast, stumbling blocks are referenced in verses where sin, disobedience, and temptation are the subject. Think about it: we trip over items that we aren't focused on. We are looking in another direction and have a misstep. Yet, when we are watching where we walk, we see the best next step to take. A sure place to rest our foot along the path—that's how it is when we focus on the Lord! He guides our steps and leads us to Him and His best plan for us.

Reflect and Respond

Map out the steppingstones in the path of your life:

Do your stones still feel like stumbling blocks, or can you see how God is a solid footing to stand on, leading you to your own redemption story?

Has your perspective about your past changed?

How can you focus your eyes on Him as he guides you to the next solid steppingstones?

DAY 27

Arise

—Katie—

> "Arise, shine, for your light has come, and the glory of the Lord has risen upon you. For behold, darkness shall cover the earth, and thick darkness the peoples; but the Lord will arise upon you, and his glory will be seen upon you. And nations shall come to your light, and kings to the brightness of your rising."
>
> Isaiah 60:1–3, ESV

Have you ever felt like you missed your chance? Or maybe you think things will always be the same and that things can't improve for someone like you. I used to think I was just bound to be a mess. I didn't think I could live up to the expectations other people had of me. So I settled and began existing instead of living. But do you know what I was truly missing out on? God's purpose for my life, fullness of joy, peace in His provision, and so much more.

You see, once I began to realize that I didn't have to fit a certain look, have the most successful career, or live the life other people said I should, I found freedom. And what I love about Jesus is that He can use anything to fulfill His purposes—even you, friend. Let's reframe Isaiah 60:1-3 to see how God loves and encourages us through His promises.

> "Arise, shine, for the light grows within you through God who lives in you. This world is full of darkness, but because of God who is in you, you will shine bright, full of His purpose in your life, and people will see it. People will want to know about the goodness of God through you" (Isaiah 60:1-3, paraphrased)

You didn't miss the mark, and it's never too late to see what God has planned for your life. I am confident that while life will still have struggles, you will rise to the identity and full potential God created you for. I'm cheering you on!

A DEVOTIONAL FOR PREGNANT WOMEN IN UNEXPECTED PLACES

Reflect and Respond

What dreams do you have for the future?

How can God be glorified through those goals?

How is God currently working in your life today?

DAY 28

Bloom Where You Are Planted

—Leah—

"But blessed is the one who trusts in the LORD, whose confidence is in him. They will be like a tree planted by the water that sends out its roots by the stream. It does not fear when heat comes; its leaves are always green. It has no worries in a year of drought and never fails to bear fruit."

Jeremiah 17:7–8, NIV

Has the Lord ever put certain people in your life at just the right time? Or does a song come on from your playlist at a time when you desperately need the message? Mrs. Dunn was that person for me when I was pregnant in high school. There were others, of course, who were my support system and helped me through this difficult time as well, but my childhood development teacher gave me the gift of encouragement. She simply took the time to be there for me, to listen impartially, and, most importantly, she let me know she believed in me no matter what I decided. One day after class, she handed me a hand-crafted card cut from magazine pages. Piecing together different letters she had spelled out, "Bloom Where You Are Planted." Glued beside her note was a picture of a watering can blooming with colorful arrangements of wildflowers. That card became a motto through the rest of my pregnancy and continues to be so to this day. It gave me the courage to keep growing no matter what circumstance I found myself in.

Friend, know that the Lord desires you to bloom where you are planted as well. The fireweed flower is an example of that in nature, as are the flowers that find roots and bloom in between the cracks of the sidewalks or stone walls! It can seem like an unlikely place to find flowers thriving, but it just takes a

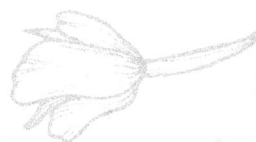

little bit of soil and water to make a seed blown in by the wind grow. No matter what you are facing today, hope can be the rays of sunshine you need to flourish. Faith in the Lord's provision can be the water your soul needs to thrive. Just like the tree planted by a stream where its roots are drawing nutrients constantly, the Lord is your living water.

> "Jesus answered, 'Everyone who drinks this water will be thirsty again, but whoever drinks the water I give them will never thirst. Indeed, the water I give them will become in them a spring of water welling up to eternal life.'"
>
> John 4:13–14, NIV

He can help you bloom right here, right in this situation, this rocky ground or burned-up valley you've found yourself in. Draw from His nutrients daily, bask in hope for your future, and He promises you will bear fruit—blessings!

Reflect and Respond

What are some ways that you can "draw nutrients" from the Lord each day?

How have you seen this to be helpful to worry less and bloom more?

List a few ways that God placed the right message, song, or person in your life to encourage you. How did these help you grow?

A DEVOTIONAL FOR PREGNANT WOMEN IN UNEXPECTED PLACES

DAY 29
He Rewrote My Story
—Katie—

"God rewrote the text of my life when I opened the book of my heart to his eyes."

Psalm 18:24 MSG

As a worship leader, I can't help but give a slow clap to the master lyricist, David the shepherd boy. But did you know he was so much more than a shepherd boy who played a harp?

Christ's lineage traces back to David through Joseph. David killed a Philistine giant named Goliath with faith and a slingshot. He was a king anointed by God. He was a mighty warrior who marched with God's strength by his side, and he wrote half of the book of Psalms.

David's life was more than this highlight reel though, and throughout Psalms you can maybe relate to his expressions of distress. He committed adultery with Bathsheba, and he plotted to kill her husband, Uriah, after he failed to get Uriah to sleep with Bathsheba to conceal his affair with her. It was one of David's low moments, so low that God stated He was displeased with David's behavior (2 Samuel 11:27). Despite all of that, God also called David "a man after [His] own heart" (Acts 13:22, NIV).

God doesn't just care about our highlight reels; He cares about the reality of it all. David is a great example of a great man who was imperfectly human but still favored by God—so much so that He made a path for David to thrive. God is making that path for me, and He is making it for you, too.

A DEVOTIONAL FOR PREGNANT WOMEN IN UNEXPECTED PLACES

Reflect and Respond

Why do you think God used David to lead Israel as their King?

Just like David, your story is more than a highlight reel. Think about the image you present to the world, your highlight reel. What is the truth?

David's story is full of redemption. How is God rewriting your story?

DAY 30

Receiving Blessings
—Leah—

"May the Lord bless you and protect you. May the Lord smile on you and be gracious to you. May the Lord show you his favor and give you his peace."
Numbers 6:24–26, NLT

When I was pregnant with my birth daughter and reading profile books to choose a family for her, there was one profile that stood out to me. It was the one where the family prayed a blessing over me, and it instantly brought me peace. What they wrote stemmed from Numbers 6:24-26, and I felt seen and cared for, not only by the parents' writing but also by the Lord. You may recognize this verse that was written into the song "The Blessing" by Cody Carnes and Kari Jobe. I highly recommend you go listen to it!

As I was praying to the Lord about how to end this book, the image of open hands came to mind, much like our book cover. At my church, our pastor speaks a benediction over us at the end of the service. Benediction simply means blessing. With cupped hands held in front of us, we receive blessing and instruction for the week ahead. It's always a short prayer directly from the Bible, but the simple words bring such a sense of peace and "filling up." After all, we can't pour out love and blessings to others—including our children—without filling our own cup up first.

We've talked a lot throughout the days of this devotional about putting our trust and hope into the Lord in whatever circumstances and decisions you are making right now. They are action steps taken in faith. Today, I pray you will cup your hands and simply receive blessings. Still your heart, mind, and your body. Pause and just receive. Know that the Lord does want to bless *you* and keep *you* in the protection of His care. Feel the warmth of love as His face shines upon you because *He delights in you!* Allow His peace to wash over you.

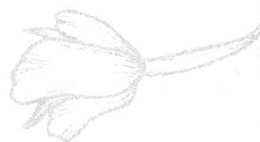

This verse can become a simple prayer to the Lord by exchanging "you" with "me." Cup your hand and receive His blessing for your life:

May the Lord bless me and protect me. May the Lord smile on me and be gracious to me. May the Lord show me His favor and give me peace.

Now, let's pray a blessing over your child's life. Fill your child's name in (if you don't have a name yet, you can put "my baby"):

May the Lord bless _____ and protect _____. May the Lord smile on _____ and be gracious to _____. May the Lord show _____ His favor and give _____ peace.

Closing letter

    Regardless of what tomorrow brings, we hope you feel worthy of motherhood, however that will look in your current journey. Remember that God isn't surprised by any of this. He has good plans for your life and for your baby's life. He will not forsake you. Keep leaning into His wisdom day by day. We pray that, as you move forward into parenting or adoption, you will feel God's loving goodness so clearly in your life and that He will guide your steps. May He bless you and your future generations with the gift of knowing Him deeply. We are so proud of you for where you are today and pray that you will cling to the Flourishing Hope of tomorrow.

    We pray the words over the last 30 days have been little seeds of hope, tucked away in the soil of your heart, and you will bloom exactly where God has planted you. You've got this, momma!

With all our love,

Katie and Leah

Acknowledgments

A book doesn't come together without the help of others throughout the process. From discussing ideas to design to edits and beta readers, many people have had their eyes on these words as we prepared them for the world. Thank you to everyone who has supported this book through time and financial pledges, along with praying for this project! Above all, we pray this book brings God glory and changes lives according to His will. We praise Him for the idea and the words and for paving the way for this book to flourish.

From Katie — Thank you to all of the people who have supported me in the different seasons of motherhood. Your encouragement, kindness, and lack of judgment will forever inspire me to love on other mothers in the same ways. Thank you to my sweet husband for always cheering me on in my 5,000 extra projects and believing that not only do they make a difference, but so do I. I am the luckiest girl to have you. To my family and friends, you always clap the loudest for me and believe in everything I do. You keep me motivated to push toward all of my goals and dreams. I love you! To my kids—motherhood, parenting, and family have always looked different for us, but we've never let that stop us from making each other a priority. Loving you has helped me understand the Father's love for us a lot more, and I am so glad that I get to spend my life cheering you on and loving you for who God created you to be. You are all my world. To my Savior, Jesus—thank You for my story and for the evidence that You never stop pursuing Your children's hearts. May my testimony carry purpose and hope as it blesses others. I'll keep planting the seed and watch You do mighty things.

From Leah — Where do you begin when you wouldn't be where you are today without the support of so many? Above all, thank You, Lord, for continuing to provide the words and path for each project You assign to me. May You bless these words for Your glory. Thank you, Katie, for asking me to join you on this journey! To my husband, who is my realist balance yet biggest cheerleader, I couldn't do this life without you. To my kids, all of whom inspired these stories and deepen my relationship with the Lord. To my parents, who continually cheer me on and support me. Thank you to my writing friends, who kept encouraging me throughout this process when I couldn't see what God was doing. As Melissa Ohden told me, "If it was easy, it would have been done before." Thank you, Codi and Kingdom Winds, for bringing another creation to life!

Resources

Worship Playlist

As we were writing, many songs related to these verses and messages came to mind, and they have helped us through difficult seasons. We collected these songs for you to listen to and cling to through your difficult times, too. Hit play and spend some time with the Lord!

Leah's Spotify Playlist: Katie's Apple Music Playlist:

Support and Stories

Love Line—a nationwide hotline for pregnant women, single moms, and families in complex situations who feel they have exhausted resources in their area. Love Line connects you to resources to get back on your feet. www.loveline.com or text 888-550-1588

Brave Love—an organization to learn more about adoption, hear birth parent stories, and connect to support post-placement. www.bravelove.org

Groups

Embrace Grace—faith-based groups available nationwide for single moms to gather in community and grow together. At the end of each semester, each mom receives a shower and is lavished with a princess day! Whether you parent or place, these groups are filled with love and support. www.embracegrace.com

The Table—a birth parent and adoptee-led post-adoption resource that offers a virtual support group for birth parents

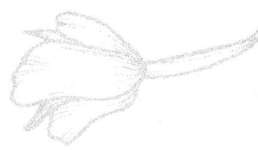

who have placed a child for adoption and in-person events in the Dallas-Fort Worth Metroplex in Texas. Find them on Facebook and Instagram @thetabledfw

BraveLove has also collected group information both online and in person for post-placement support. www.bravelove.org/post_adoption_support

Books

Praying Through Your Pregnancy: An Inspirational Week-by-Week Guide for Moms-to-Be by Jennifer Polimino and Carolyn Warren

A Bump in Life by Amy Ford

Parenthood Unplanned: A Survival Guide for the Unexpected by Sarah Dunford

The Sixteenth Year: An Open Adoption Memoir by Leah Outten

Fireweed by Jennifer Mae

Through Adopted Eyes by Elena Hall

Through Adopted Hearts by Elena Hall

Revealing You: A Journal for Birthmothers by Michelle Thorne

Adoption Picture Books for Children

The ABC's of Adoption by Raquel McCloud

Tell Me My Story: What Does Adopted Mean? by Raquel McCloud

The ABC's of Foster and Kinship Care by Raquel McCloud

Sam's Sister by Juliet C. Bond

Adoption is Both by Elena Hall

About Us

Katie McCoy is a birth mother who has placed two children for adoption. Her oldest is 17, and her youngest is 14. She has a very open adoption with them both and has enjoyed watching them flourish throughout the years. She is married and is parenting a newborn daughter. While her story hasn't always felt hopeful, she looks back on the immeasurable goodness and grace that God has bestowed on her life. He truly has used her story to speak to mothers of all walks. She has an organization with another birth mother called The Table DFW that supports men and women who have placed a child(ren) for adoption through support groups and in-person events. Katie's story has been featured on podcasts like Birth Mothers Amplified and The Open Adoption Project, featured on BraveLove's storytelling platforms, and in self-written articles on Adoption.com. Along with being a birth mother, Katie was adopted as a child and has had an open adoption with her biological family for 14 years now.

Instagram: @katiedee_88; @thetabledfw

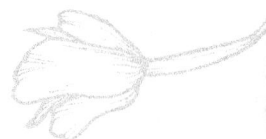

Leah Outten is a birth mother in a fully open adoption of over 20 years and a mother of 5 whom she parents with her husband. She has been writing, speaking, and serving in the adoption and pro-life communities since 2004. Her passion for helping others blossoms from the light found within the dark trenches of her life and the support surrounding her. Sharing vulnerably about the beauty and aches of a birth mother, she aims to inspire hope and healing. Leah's writing and story have been featured on national platforms, including Focus On The Family, Epoch Times, LiveAction, and HuffPost. Her memoir *The Sixteenth Year* was published in 2023.

Website: leahoutten.com

Instagram: @leahoutten

Facebook: facebook.com/thegracebond